Dependencies

D1600629

Dependencies

Poems

LISEL MUELLER

LOUISIANA STATE UNIVERSITY PRESS • BATON ROUGE

Louisiana Paperback Edition, 1998
07 06 05 04 03 02 01 00 99 98   5 4 3 2 1

Library of Congress Cataloging-in-Publication Data

Mueller, Lisel.
    Dependencies : poems / Lisel Mueller. —Louisiana pbk. ed.
        p.   cm.
    ISBN 0-8071-2275-0 (alk. paper)
    I. Title.
    PS3563.U35D4   1998
    811'.54—dc21   97-46684
                                                         CIP

"In Memory of Anton Webern," "Nine Months Making," "Sunlight and Shadow," "In the Thriving Season," "The Bride's Complaint," "Afterthoughts on the Lovers," "The Mermaid," "Bach Transcribing Vivaldi," "The Siege," "The Expense of Spirit in a Waste of Shame" (published as "A Long Way from Hell"), "A Prayer for Rain," "The Blind Leading the Blind," "Cicadas," and "The Poem of Love" originally appeared in *Poetry*. The poems "The Queen of Sheba Says Farewell," "A Grackle Observed," "On Finding a Bird's Bones in the Woods," "Sunday Fishing," and "The Lonesome Dream" appeared originally in *The New Yorker*. Other poems were originally published in *The Saturday Review, The Sewanee Review, Perspective, The Quarterly Review of Literature, The Fiddlehead, Dimension: Cincinnati, The Christian Century*, and *The New Orleans Poetry Journal*. Some of the poems in this volume have been reprinted in the following anthologies: *New Poems by American Poets #2, Best Poems of 1958, The Various Light*, and *Best Articles and Stories*.

For Paul

We live in an old chaos of the sun,
Or old dependency of day and night,
Or island solitude, unsponsored, free,
Of that wide water, inescapable.

—WALLACE STEVENS

Contents

Dependencies

The Blind Leading The Blind

Take my hand. There are two of us in this cave.
The sound you hear is water; you will hear it forever.
The ground you walk on is rock. I have been here before.
People come here to be born, to discover, to kiss,
to dream and to dig and to kill. Watch for the mud.
Summer blows in with scent of horses and roses;
fall with the sound of sound breaking; winter shoves
its empty sleeve down the dark of your throat.
You will learn toads from diamonds, the fist from the palm,
love from the sweat of love, falling from flying.
There are a thousand turnoffs. I have been here before.
Once I fell off a precipice. Once I found gold.
Once I stumbled on murder, the thin parts of a girl.
Walk on, keep walking, there are axes above us.
Watch for occasional bits and bubbles of light—
birthdays for you, recognitions: *yourself, another.*
Watch for the mud. Listen for bells, for beggars.
Something with wings went crazy against my chest once.
There are two of us here. Touch me.

In The Thriving Season
In memory of my mother

Now as she catches fistfuls of sun
riding down dust and air to her crib,
my first child in her first spring
stretches bare hands back to your darkness
and heals your silence, the vast hurt
of your deaf ear and mute tongue
with doves hatched in her young throat.

Now ghost-begotten infancies
are the marrow of trees and pools
and blue uprisings in the woods
spread revolution to the mind,
I can believe birth is fathered
by death, believe that she was quick
when you forgave pain and terror
and shook the fever from your blood.

Now in the thriving season of love
when the bud relents into flower,
your love turned absence has turned once more,
and if my comforts fall soft as rain
on her flutters, it is because
love grows by what it remembers of love.

The Siege

Once, when he was away, across the sea
and she intent on tears and broken sleep,
the afternoon in which another played
the keyboard for her, softened and grew deep;
persuasions lifted from the air of love
fingered the curtain and slipped past the chair,
twilight of grape and burgundy of rose
washed out the ceiling, swam against her hair:

O, since he was away and she in love
with hints and echoes, love's sweet stock in trade,
she slowly fell into the mossy lap
of that near-darkness, where another played
and forced her dreams like early hyacinths
that open in the April of a room—
and made no move to call the velvet bluff,
so willing was she to endure that bloom.

Bach Transcribing Vivaldi

One remembered the sunrise, how clearly it gave
substance and praise to the mountains of the world;
the other imagined twilight, the setting in blood,
and a valley of fallen leaves where a stranger might rest.

One avoided the forest and made his way through fields
where the sky was constant and clouds rang in his ears;
the other cut through the thicket, the thorns and vines
and was not touched, except by the dying of men.

One asked the road to the land of the golden lion
whose eyes never weep, whose lifted hand scepters
the seasons of stars and the grafting of generations;
the other searched for the kingdom of the lamb
with the trembling fleece, whose live unreasoning heart
consumes the mortal treasure of his loves.

Still, at one point of the journey one must have seen
the afternoon dip and drop away into shade
and the other come to a place where the forest cleared
into white and violet patches of stars.

The Fall

The first they knew the curve of Paradise
was when they lost it, when the toxic fruit
shared by two children, burned their childhood
 down,
when they could feel its succulence dilute
and pass into the memory's crucible,
there to be tampered with and suffer change
and punish the persistence of their tongues
with an insurgence of the tart and strange:

and when they lay, accomplished as the dead,
holding each other's beauty like a stone
aimed at their frailty, when their new-found
 need
for one another, left each one alone:

o love, that was the night their shadows grew,
monsters that rise against me, against you.

"More Light"

(Words attributed to Goethe on his deathbed)

For my father

He, too, went down on occasion,
touched land on the pitch-black bottom
of fish that can do without eyes,
tangled with spiny and slimy life,
with creatures all greedy feelers,
all sting, strike, suction,
unknown to moonlight. There must have been times
when there seemed no end to coral gardens
and the imperturbable waving of sea fans
while clamor he had not thought possible
pressed on his eardrums its rhythms
of rancorless lust. To think,
when he pleasure-sailed on the Adriatic
—August afternoons—
atop a mirror that gave of nothing
but his sure, shaved face
and an indestructible sky,
how thin that surface, how impudent!
Salons, of course, and claret and ladies with taste;
walks and sonatas and careful conversations
that could be printed verbatim;
unflinching eyes and a statesman's profile:
but there was restless Werther
and hell-bent, curious Faust.
He must have been there, gone back
to explore the secret canals
of succulent sponges, to drift
by the faint luminescence of stripes,
to let his conscience slip off
in the subtleties of the dark.
But always the clean, sharp hurt
of remembered sunlight pulled him
clear of a mermaid's breast
toward a place where men try to prove
by courtesy and equations
and by occasional mercy
that there are lovelier creatures
and more delicate pearls.

Nine Months Making

Nine months making
the pulse and tissue of love
work knowledge upon us;
the hard squeeze against bone
makes radical trial
of love's primal claim:
here in the body truth grows palpable.

Long comprehended, never
till now understood, the ancient analogy
of sap in the root as impulse
toward flowering, as drive and push
toward all possibility,
is proven upon us. Mind
tried and failed; it is body
secretes the slow-spun pearl
we say is knowledge, oystered
in our infinitely expanding
one-man and one-woman world.

Knowledge of act, not cause.
Love's wine has been our blood
for years; we shall not know
what word or weather thickened
the familiar flux, quickened
old essence into separateness of flesh.
Change and astonishment
witnessed upon my body and your eyes
these long fall evenings
unhand the shape, not mystery, of love.

Nor need we know
more than these sweetly growing pains
which are enough to publish
love's increasing refusal
to lie with the biblical dust of our bones.

The Power Of Music To Disturb

A humid night. Mad June bugs dash themselves
against a window they should know is there;
I hear an owl awaking in the woods
behind our house, and wonder if it shakes
sleep from its eyes and lets its talons play,
stretch and retract, rehearsing for the kill—
and on the radio the music drives
toward death by love, for love, because of love
like some black wave that cannot break itself.

It is a music that luxuriates
in the impossibilities of love
and rides frustration till two ghosts become
alive again, aware of how the end
of every act of love is separateness;
raw, ruthless lovers, desperate enough
to bank on the absurdity of death
for royal consummation, permanence
of feeling, having, knowing, holding on.

My God, he was a devil of a man
who wrote this music so voluptuous
it sucks me in with possibilities
of sense and soul, of pity and desire
which place and time make ludicrous: I sit
across from you here in our living room
with chairs and books and red geraniums
and ordinary lamplight on the floor
after an ordinary day of love.

How can disaster be so beautiful?
I range the beaches of our lucid world
against that flood, trying to think about
our child upstairs, asleep with her light on
to keep her from vague evils; about us
whose loving has become so natural

that it has rid itself of teeth and claws,
implements for the lovers new at love,
whose jitters goad them into drawing blood.

But o my love, I cannot beat it back,
neither the sound nor what the sound lets loose;
the opulence of agony drowns out
the hard, dry smack of death against the glass
and batters down the sea walls of my mind,
and I am pulled to levels below light
where easy ways of love are meaningless
and creatures feel their way along the dark
by shock of ecstasy and heat of pain.

On Finding A Bird's Bones
In The Woods

Even Einstein, gazing
at the slender ribs of the world,
examining and praising
the cool and tranquil core
under the boil and burning
of faith and metaphor—
even he, unlearning
the bag and baggage of notion,
must have kept some shred
in which to clothe that shape,
as we, who cannot escape
imagination, swaddle
this tiny world of bone
in all that we have known
of sound and motion.

Cicadas

Always in unison, they are
the rapt voice of silence,

so singleminded I cannot tell
if the sound is rich or thin,

cannot tell even if it is sound,
the high, sustained note

which gives to a summer field
involved with the sun at noon

a stillness as palpable
as smoke and mildew,

know only: when they are gone
one scrubbed autumn day

after the clean sweep
of the bright, acrid season,

what remains is a clearing of rest,
of balance and attention

but not the second skin,
hot and close, of silence.

The Mermaid

All day he had felt her stirring
under the boat, and several times
when the net had tightened, frog-nervous,
he had bungled the pulling-in,
half-glad of the stupid, open mouths
he could throw back.
        At sundown
the shifting and holding of time and air
had brought her to the still surface,
to sun herself in the last, slow light
where lilies and leeches tangled and rocked.
He could have taken her then, aimed his net
as dragonfly hunters do when the glassy gliding
of rainbows goes to their heads,
could have carried her home on tiptoe
and lifted her lightly, ever so lightly,
over his sill.
        And, hopeless, knew
that to have her alive was only this:
the sounding, casting, waiting, seeing
and willing the light not to move,
not yet to round the bay of her shoulder
and, passing, release her
to the darkness he would not enter.

Moon Fishing

When the moon was full they came to the water,
some with pitchforks, some with rakes,
some with sieves and ladles
and one with a silver cup.

And they fished till a traveler passed them and said,
"Fools,
to catch the moon you must let your women
spread their hair on the water—
even the wily moon will leap to that bobbing
net of shimmering threads,
gasp and flop till its silver scales
lie black and still at your feet."

And they fished with the hair of their women
till a traveler passed them and said,
"Fools,
do you think the moon is caught lightly,
with glitter and silk threads?
You must cut out your hearts and bait your hooks
with those dark animals;
what matter you lose your hearts to reel in your dream?"

And they fished with their tight, hot hearts
till a traveler passed them and said,
"Fools,
what good is the moon to a heartless man?
Put back your hearts and get on your knees
and drink as you never have,
until your throats are coated with silver
and your voices ring like bells."

And they fished with their lips and tongues
until the water was gone
and the moon had slipped away
in the soft, bottomless mud.

Sans Souci

(Frederick the Great's summer palace near Potsdam)

It does not make sense in terms of historical fact,
the unabashed gesture, the celebration of joy,
birds that catch and diffract
the afternoon sun and drink from a bubbling nymph
who beckons a marble boy;

nor the make-believe heaven inside: golden frames
looping their spiraling curls about mirrors that blaze
whirlpools of light on the games
of Arcadian lovers dappling a celadon wall;
yet we might have expected it. Praise

is the louder and passion the fiercer for need,
fiercest when bred in a mind that has knelt to a whip
and recanted its natural creed
of splendor and bliss. Rigidity once removed
is freedom and grace, and the tight-stretched line of
     a lip

curves to the flute's convolutions of silver and breath.
But for the hair that we split in order to prove
otherwise, death
reverses to motion and sunlight. Turned inside-out,
negation is equal to love.

A Grackle Observed

Watching the black grackle
come out of the gray shade
into the sun, I am dazzled
by an unsuspected sheen,
yellow, purple, and green,
where the comb of light silkens
unspectacular wings—
until he, unaware
of what he means at this one
peculiar angle of sun,
hops back to his modest dark
and leaves the shining part
of himself behind, as though
brightness must outgrow
its fluttering worldly dress
and enter the mind outright
as vision, as pure light.

The Lonesome Dream

In the America of the dream
the first rise of the moon
swings free of the ocean,
and she reigns in her shining flesh
over a good, great valley
of plumed, untrampled grasses
and beasts with solemn eyes,
of lovers infallibly pitched
in their ascendant phase.

In this America, death
is virginal also, roaming
the good, great valley
in his huge boots, his shadow
steady and lean, his pistol
silver, his greeting clear
and courteous as a stranger's
who looks for another, a mind
to share his peaceable evenings.

Dreaming, we are another
race than the one which wakes
in the cold sweat of fear,
fires wild shots at death,
builds slippery towers of glass
to head him off, waylays him
with alcohol traps, rides him down
in canyons of sex, and hides
in teetering ghost towns.

Dreaming, we are the mad
who swear by the blood of trees
and speak with the tongues of streams
through props of steel and sawdust;
a colony of souls
ravaged by visions, bound
to some wild, secret cove
not yet possessed, a place
still innocent of us.

The Queen Of Sheba Says Farewell

Sir, as one royal personage to another,
let me confess that I am sick for home.
I came to test you with the hardest questions
my Ministers could devise in their sessions
of finger-tapping, table-drumming, placing
their index fingers flat against their noses
for more incisive thought. You answered all,
spelling, besides, each complicated word
in their black dictionaries, and so gained
rights to my bed. *Noblesse oblige;* this is
proper and as it should be.

               I regret
nothing, but did not come for love—rather,
to shame you out of pride. Do you remember
how many trunks of ivory my camels
carried? One hundred elephants gave up
their eyeteeth to accommodate my need
to show you up with riches. I had hoped
to humble you with slabs of beaten gold
and openwork done by my master craftsmen,
stun you with scents of oils and precious spices,
and catch you like a brazen fly, only
to drown you in the honey of my scorn.
I failed in this, too. Solomon, I now
offer my gifts in all humility,
praising your patience.

               Still, I must go home.
Your wisdom cloys, or is beginning to;
proverbial pearls lose their luster in time.
I am uncomfortable when your scribes
doodle on their blank tablets, poised to pounce
on any utterance you care to make—
the bones you throw posterity. I long
for nervous jungle drums on these occasions,
am tempted to defy you with a dance
unseemly here. And I dislike the stare

of golden oxen in my bath; my own
taste runs to water lilies whose white faces
move with my motion.

                    Let us be quite frank—
we do not suit each other, though your songs
almost persuaded me. O Solomon,
my love, my tongue of tongueless cherubim,
I shall not sleep again without your songs
deep in my ears! On long, hot evenings,
I'll teach my slaves the music of those words.
I am not a wise, just queen, not an enlightened
          monarch—
rather, a noble savage, quick to beat
my sad black dancers, quick to be afraid.
I fear my loneliness; I have seen lions
observe me in my hammock from the edge
of darkness after sundown. But I am sick
for my own country, where my clapping hands
command an almond tree to rise and bloom
behind my ear, and ebony girls come
and whisper to me of their love affairs.
Spring is sweeter there.

                    I shall not come again.

The People At The Party

They are like tightrope walkers, unable to fall
from the precise thread of their making,
having achieved the most delicate of all
balances of the brain, which is forsaking

joy on the one hand, and on the other, terror;
holding themselves exquisitely aloof
from the contingencies of love and error,
they dare nothing, are wholly removed

by the will not to suffer, from us who do.
Ah, but they are precariously perched
on their rope of detachment. Who
can be sure someone improperly coached

won't say the wrong word or turn back
the cruel joke with a human response?
That the only girl not in serpent black
will keep her distance? There is always a chance

someone careless or young will unsettle the
    cable,
bring on the vertigo and set them reeling
toward the sheer drop, toward the unstable
inexorable wilderness of feeling.

Sunday Fishing

Another minor jungle has been cleared,
tenuous lattices of light and shade
bulldozed from memory, shy things expelled
toward a stop-gap refuge, some last ditch
of secrecy, so we may park and pay
for public leisure under blasts of sun
in a brand-new, two-acre wonderland
where red and yellow candy wrappers toss
in the displeasure of a dirty wind.

Even the bite is fixed. The trout that stock
the baby blue of these invented streams
know better than to try and get away;
they shame us by compliance, come in droves
as if to mock the old prerogatives
which used to let us gamble on our luck
and test our patience under willow trees
while watching all the humors of the sky—
in on the game, these creatures gulp and die.

Tires spin and screech, as bright, insensate fins
threaten each other in their push to church
along the highway, a few feet from us:
what fool thought he could give us Paradise
with gravel walks and whittled redwood signs
and paid-for guarantees? Already flawed,
this garden galls what innocence we have—
let's throw the rainbows back and take a chance
along some godforsaken country creek.

Eros

An apple-cheeked little boy,
he discovered his free-wheeling mother
one afternoon with Adonis
under the olive trees,
and wandered away inspired
to his own precocious game,
a child's variation, the thrill
of making something happen—
of spying, secretly stinging,
altering, being the cause
of weddings and backstairs murders,
of women breaking their hearts
and men blowing on dreams:

and wondering all the time
(this boy who never grew up)
what it was all about,
why a thing that begins
as sheer delight, mere play,
turns on itself, turns inward,
puts spells and threats on time,
fire, air, and all the dead,

why the heart, tight in its skin,
demands to be stripped naked
and then hides out in terror
because it has no disguise,

why, why, why
this springing up of gardens
and cities and poems and gods,
as still another man
and another woman bring down
the burden of love on themselves.

In Praise Of Morning

For my sister

Bless the anatomist
that severs the cotton of sleep
into separate sounds and things,

bless clarity, bless air
split into ripsaws, brakes,
bare feet and flapping wings

as the soft noose of the night,
the leash of stars and sadness,
drops like a snake's dead skin

and the sparrow atop the hawthorn
stretches its white-streaked throat
and whistles *begin, begin.*

Jazz At Newport

For Carol

1. Drummer

I know my love
he said and laid
a lover's hands
on parchment white
and held his breath
and was obeyed
by a slow pulse
of doomed delight
 I know the slut
 he cried and cut
 the fleeing sound
 off in mid-air
 and swung around
 and swung a pair
 of rabid sticks
 on the white sheath
 and shut his eyes
 and gnashed his teeth
  I know my love
  and she is dead
  his dry lips said
  and his brown hands
  lay damp, outspread
  on the white head

2. Girl in a Red Sweater

Bottle raised like a horn
sweet and straight to the moon
 she dances seaward, tipsy
 with beer and voodoo, legs
 in levis monkey-supple,
bare toes tracking
animal signs through sand,

eyelids fallen petals,
mouth in this light black
around the mouth of the bottle,
rope-thin, rope-strong the arm
that turns an imagined windmill
as she arrives and swings
—o bull's-eye, be, be real!—
and the hot bottle flies
spins shines falls
on the hard slap of water.

For Lucy

(The Cuban Crisis, October 1962)

While I was cowed and still
before the war which trained
its death on you, us, all,
you inveighed against wolves
and witches, worked up nerve
to go to your dark bed.

Our difference was one of kind
and metaphor, otherwise
we dreaded the same thing;
for me, as for you, dying
is being caught once only,
even en masse, alone.

So you painted a witch's face
and we taped it to the door
and cut a skeleton grin
into a pumpkin head
and let it burn on the porch
to keep off the real thing.

Dear ceremonial child:
so far, so good; Halloween
has come and gone, and you
are still as beautiful.
Magic? Who knows, who knows
what rites persuade our luck:

But I have ears sharpened
by an age of evil news
and still hear high-pitched howls
which love cannot outcry;
one-handed I touch you,
the other touches wood.

A Plain Sonnet

To tell of Pharaoh's daughter by the stream
or Jacob's stolen blessing, is to tell
the sum of being. Still, we guard the dream
of our uniqueness like a citadel,
as though our age were winnowed from the rest
to try out all the latitudes of hell,
all aspects of the rack, chosen to test
the breaking point. Convinced that we excel
in complex agony, we forget that pain
is simple and regardless of its cause
an absolute, forget that to arouse
love from its chronic sickbed and sustain
it through the age until the age unbend,
was mind's beginning and will be its end.

Figure For A Landscape

Look, the solitary walker
out on this coldest Sunday of the year
shoulders the whole burden of the fable
which winter is, the moral panorama
of a silence so vast that all sounds have meaning.

In summer the landscape was simply
itself, and concealment humanly possible
in grass and shadow and the living noise
of child singers and animal dancers,
baroque in their cultivation of opulence

and the green life. But now
even the lake is petrified out of sound,
and the sky, impartially plundered
of inessential leaves, birds, clouds,
throws back his face without kindly distortion

as though he alone could answer for winter.
The tracks of the dead and the dying accost him,
crossing his footprints wherever he walks,
stands, is alive; and the clamor of ice
comes down with a crash, like an unstruck bell,

splitting his ears. In this season,
while we stay home with coffee and morning
newspapers, sensible of the danger
confronting us in the sight of a branch
gloved by a child's lost mitten,

he is the hero who bears all loss,
who, by no particular virtue
other than solitude, takes on himself
the full silence, the whole terrible
knowledge the landscape no longer conceals.

Modern Romance

For Felix

Love's levelling took place
in the brightest spot by the side of the road,
and afterwards princess and swineherd
played the same tune on their common flute.

Forevers said, they built
their gold-and-silver palace,
circled their string of rooms once a day,
played Jacks with their duller diamonds
when the time grew long between drinks.

And when they found the old cheat, love,
had gone over the hill,
he in his counting-house, she in her parlor,
made hay while the sun still shone—
then she upstaged him in a glitter of tears,
calling goodbye from the public garden
of frankly staring statues,
while he faded into his separate sunset.

Apology

He was my early love, come
    from the hazy hill of the world
    to give my formless fever
    a cause, a name, a sickness:

    my gentle love; bird
    in the limbs and twigs of his comforts
    I skipped and fluttered before hawk's pride
    speared and stiffened my wings:

    my handy love, carpenter
    of my open, jigsawed house,
    potter of silences, shepherd of secrets,
    diamond-cutter of idleness:

    my first, best, chaste, lost love,
    prince of all weather, jack of all dreams,
    and I deny him, scorn him, mock him,
    refuse him pity, call him fool
    lest he return—o dove, o serpent!—
    unchanged for all my stone years.

The Bride's Complaint

I saw the face of my love naked
and that was more than my love could bear—
o red-eyed bull of the sun,
how many times must I cross you?

My kisses are petals past his mouth
and sparrows twitter away my breath—
whirligig world, run slow, run down,
let my love remember me!

The Poem Of Love

Not about her who turns dancer
in the space he illumines by waiting,
not about his leaping impatience
which praises the dust of her lightness—
but about the contender, the brilliant third
who trips them and drives them away
to watch him from separate wings:

Not about words fetched and carried
like fruit from one to the other,
not about moments that gush from unorthodox
    light
and settle into the landscape—
but about words that the wind bites off,
moments burned out in expectation
arriving piecemeal, dead.

Not about night and the bridge
it stretches from runner to runner,
not about sexual grace—
but about the chink between lovers,
wide enough for the swallow that whistles good-
    bye
to shiver into and wait out the storm
of their forgetful embracing:

If about love at all,
then about love in another country
or love imagined to music—
more often about things missing or broken,
the boomerang of desire, the heart's disrepair,
the shakedown after the spell.
It is not written by lovers.

The Homecoming

1.

I had forgotten dew
was the sweat of morning

I had forgotten birds wage war
over a scrawny blackberry

I had forgotten sumacs,
tough as rowdy cocks,
showed their blood so early

I had forgotten how sun
thrusts its thorns in my eyes
and the posse of roofs
converging, closing in

I had forgotten that words
are part salt, part thunder

2.

I was the pet of keepers
who rocked and coddled my terrors,
swept them under my eyelids
and put them to sleep in my veins.
Dreaming among dreamers
I was allowed to groom
experience, comb out
tangles of noise and pain.
Here I am lost: this road,
which is to take me home,
takes me away. You ride
some great joy like a mare
and I behind you stretch
the feelers of my mind
after so live a thing
and draw back stung, unnerved.

My toddling shadow, trying,
cannot catch up with yours.

3.

In that closed vacuum,
contagion of forgetting,
my memory renounced
the tumult of our bed,
the laborings of pleasure
and seizures of the flesh—
all but the wishlessness,
the stillness afterwards
which enthralls the muscular lion
at the quivering heart of the world
and stays the wars of motion
for the span of a lovers' lull:
                                    O lost kingdom,
where colors faded politely
—dusk amethyst, stone green,
gray spun by noiseless spiders,
reticent, sheer as dust—
where walls and scentless hedges
kept out the peeping seasons,
the thick of cries and kisses,
and strangers, fellow-strangers,
grew intimate through a curtain
of ceremonies: suppers,
cards, occasional dances
under endurable stars,
world and light enough
for my small, floating joys.

4.

If by return you mean
that I must learn again
the savage and the strange,

if you must bring me back
as one more dancer, steeped
in the intrigues of change,

if I must celebrate
the odds of flight and fall
that will upend my praise,

then let me see the cause
extravagant enough
unriddled in your gaze

and let your voice assume
my tunelessness, until
I call this journey good:

lost face, face of my love
turn and be recognized,
look and be understood.

Sunrise In The Heart
Of Darkness
(The Congo, 1961)

All the while the stake
rotted, the tender body
of wood giving way to time's
forgiveness of wind and rain,
the shrunken head endured,
prospered, fleshed itself,
gathered and stored pain
in its hollows, made cheeks and eyes
from layered crusts of hate—
until the jocose dream
that smiled and smiled in the jaws
and fed on spoilage, sprang
its bony trap and flashed
the sign for the dawn to break
in a glittering sac of blood.

Woman With Chrysanthemum

Doggedly she has come through the fall,
her broken beauties a light load;
only the stalk is left to wither.

Softness went first. The green curl
of budding darkened, toughened, grew
harder to crush in the wind's fingers.

Flower next, the bold show,
its sex awake in the male sun,
its bend and sway rooted in darkness.

Only the hardy stalk, herself
past heyday and ripeness still endures:
essential bone, primeval spirit.

Why should she care or be afraid?
After such measurements of loss
death is only one more dying.

Sunlight And Shadow

"But Italy worked some marvel on her. It gave her light, and—which he held more precious—it gave her shadow . . . "

E. M. Forster, A Room with a View

1.

Watch any cool Northern girl
renounce her clean transparency
in this strenuous light;
shadowless until now, her edge of being
defined by her skirt, she stands in the noon piazza
seeking asylum from sun, half-afraid
of the stone naves and transepts,
the vaulted fountains
where darkness broods; half-afraid
to fathom her own rich well, feel her mind
fall, fall to the unguessed bottom
of blood and rhythm,
where life begins.

2.

What a pity, said Miss Bartlett, *that Botticelli
spoiled a lovely scene by that unfortunate nude;*
while her young cousin, swooning with a strange joy,
fell into a thicket of violets
and was kissed by a man.
Pity Miss Bartlett. But Lucy,
groping her depth, as yet merely sensing it,
like a woman sick at the smell of fish
and ignorant still of the cause,
blamed too much Beethoven and the onslaught
of heaving violets.

3.

Leonardo's
angels and saints look like women; remember

the seraph with hair like a girl's, and the Baptist's
softly curved arm, his delicately fleshed hand
pointing toward his lips where mysterious dancers
cluster in corners. We speak of the smile,
but it is more: it is light and shadow
balanced to love, and the woman fondling her weasel
knows all about the feel of the sun
on each single point of his stretching fur.

4.

What begins in the dark shall come into sunlight,
from infancy under the threshold of knowledge,
from massed unawareness, into the orbit
of ferreting sun, acclaim
the existence of self. Take any act of creation,
in the tumbling mind of sensuous Leonardo,
in the marriage-bed—can you say where it starts?
The bees are absent all winter, yet dance
more accurately than the barometer shows
the movement of summer's light
toward glistening honey.

First Snow In Lake County

All night it fell around us
as if the sky had been sheared,
its fleece dropping forever
past our windows, until our room
was as chaste and sheltered
as Ursula's, where she lay
and dreamed herself in heaven:
and in the morning we saw
that the vision had held, looked out
on such a sight as we wish for
all our lives:
a thing, place, time
untouched and uncorrupted,
the world before we were here.

Even the wind held its peace.

And already, as our eyes
hung on, hung on, we longed
to make that patience bear
our tracks, already our daughter
put on her boots and screamed,
and the dog jumped with the joy
of splashing the white with yellow
and digging through the snow
to the scents and sounds below.

Afterthoughts On The Lovers

I imagine them always in summer,
with roses running a loose-lipped hazard
around their book, as butterflies
poised in the net of noon:
I think of her silent, wholly brought
under siege by his voice, staring
confusion down to the marble squares,
hearing and trying not to hear
how sweetly Lancelot plagued the queen.

What if they had outlived
their full-bloom summer, had dwindled
into the blight of autumn
and trees shedding their leaves
had brought them dreams, such dreams—
if mind on the prowl for flesh
had set its teeth on love
and pointed fingers at their furtiveness?

What if no violence
had sealed their immortality
for us, who need to think of love
as a fixed sun, impervious to our passing
in and out of the shade?

Rookery: Brookfield Zoo

One came forth
from the jumble of beaks and feathers
and flew past the towering lights,
his outsize keepers,
into the lawless dark

and came back singing,
unsteady with the delight
of having discovered danger,
the secret garden,

and tumbling above the crowd
shrilled his incredible tidings
over and over, as if
those grounded ears could hear,
those soft bellies rise.

"O Brave New World,
That Hath Such People In It"

Soon you will be like her, Prospero's daughter,
finding the door that leads out of yourself;
out of the rare, enameled ark of your mind,
where you live with the gracious and light-footed
    creatures
that thrive in the glaze of your art and freedom.

Soon you will see the face, child, of a man
with its ridges and slopes, its cisterns of natural light;
you will wander by streams across the plain of a hand,
envy the dark as it lies down on a shoulder,
and for the sake of that shoulder, that hand, that face

banish yourself from the one flawless place.

Suspension Bridge: Twilight

The smoking, rusting beast
—our green ankylosaurus—

refines itself to a hum
between these silver strands

hammered for an imagined
woman's white-knuckled wrist

—a lady's rather, small,
slenderly old-fashioned,

the wrist of one who delights
in such sherbet sunsets

as this one in raspberry, filched
from a romance. Yet we bump

ashore in another part
of the land, and looking back

see her stand unbroken,
swaying only a little

as if she felt, too late,
the weight of our bon voyage.

The Cremona Violin
(After E. T. A. Hoffmann's story)

Two red spots on Antonia's cheeks
gave early warning. So her father-lover,
swearing that she should never
sing again, took down the violin
Amati or perhaps Guarneri made,
as proxy for her voice.

Evenings he played, doors shut to company.
Then her breath rose, eyes glistened, muscles tensed
until, fatigued, she took
a low bow and cried out,
"I never was better, father;
how well you make me sing!"

Priceless to him, those evenings with his daughter
whom neither the world nor another lover
should ever claim again.
Now that she was his instrument,
he learned new subleties of playing,
new ways of tenderness.

And killed her with that playing. Her flawed chest
could not abide love's labor. When she died
he broke the singing body into bits,
and hung a cypress wreath
where it had been, and danced
a dance of death, his black crape flying.

The Midnight Child

Then the moon threw pebbles
on the small boy's window
and took him past sleeping dogs
into the night of black roses
and small shivers of grass.

Into the shoreless night.
Through faceless wax daisies,
through clover, hint of honey
in the drained, bleached fields.
To the edge of the woods, and there
to wait in weeds and shadows.

His cheeks still warm with kisses.
And when the beast came out
between the trees, all hide,
all claws, all bloodshot eyes,
the child was not afraid.
And would have left that place
quiet and sure, until
he saw the beast slip off
his hairy skin, become
a gathering of whiteness
and small shivers of flesh,
a naked human shape
alone and ignorant
in a thin patch of light.

And then the cry, the child's
runaway voice, the heart
wild in the net of the moon.

Noli Me Tangere

Leave me, she said to me,
you will not find in my murdered flesh
a tooth or hair of death;
though you breathe into my mouth
with your incessant whys
I will not give death away.

You shall not twist my bones
into a star's shape, nor plant my hair
as roots for the dreams of the living;
and if you open my heart
and run your poet's fingers
over its walls and cushions
you will find it is like yours,
dark.

Leave me, she said,
said her slayer, said
the Negro boy in the river,
said the bureaucrat of the ovens,
said the millions in cattle graves,

leave us.

The Annunciation

Dusk was the angel, as she sat under
  the gray stone arch, feeling tender

toward the creatures of evening; rabbit and plover
  coming to drink from her jug, never

before so tame. The sun had dropped to its burrow
  behind the hill, and the narrow

virgin body of iris withdrawn in its sheath,
  though roses were still spread beneath

the love of bees. The patient jaws of silence
  swallowed stray noises, and distance,

like dreams and water, retreated beyond itself,
  leaving her marginless, half-

willing to run from the hovering mystery
  (thieflike in shadow, till she

should say, *approach and enter into my mind*).
  Dusk was the angel. She found

her courage and bid him deliver the word
  gently, gently. But when she heard

the rush of his wings, she cried, *God, God,*
  at the encroaching sky, and the child

in her womb was made quick at the name.
  Then she knew all. The angel went as he came.

A Holy Madness

*"Be praised, my Lord, for brother wind, and
for air and cloud, calms and all weather by
which you give substance to your creatures."*

St. Francis of Assissi

To say *thou* to the sun
and call the wind brother;
to be humble before a grain of sand
and speak familiarly to the sea;
to preach to the birds in earnest
as though a word were a crumb;
to give one's coat to a shorn lamb
and warm the cold with one's breath—
o holy love, sweet lunacy,
which of us, seeing a child
exhorting a deaf robin,
does not bless that child
for the paradise in his head?

To pity the low-slung valleys
and warn the hills of pride;
to address the stars by their given names
and trouble the oak for its shade;
to entrust one's doubts to the snow
and one's prospects to the grass—
which of us, watching the child
growing toward the season
when his eyes shall be opened,
would not stitch up the rip
in the single cloth of the world?

Be praised, my Lord, for Francis,
brother to lilies, be praised:
he was our brother too.

Ecology: The Lion

Let me illustrate by way of example
from history, from the last war:
when the city burned that day, that night,
those many days and nights, the flames
finally bit through the bars of his cage
and set him free. He was wary of freedom
at first, of its charred, black taste. But the fire
drove him out of the zoo and eastward,
and his confidence grew in the burned-out streets
where children stuck to the boiling asphalt;
heat urged his soles like the native heat
of his rampant days, and when he reached
the river, spurred by sounds of panic
breaking through leafage of smoke,
he felt easy enough to stand still
and savor the scent of catastrophe
that welcomed him like a greeting from home.

A Prayer For Rain

Let it come down: these thicknesses of air
have long enough walled love away from love;
stillness has hardened until words despair
of their high leaps and kisses shut themselves
back into wishing. Crippled lovers lie
against a weather that holds out on them,
waiting, awaiting some shrill sign, some cry,
some screaming cat that smells a sacrifice
and spells them thunder. Start the mumbling lips,
syllable by monotonous syllable,
that wash away the sullen griefs of love
and drown out knowledge of an ancient war:

o ill-willed dark, give with the sound of rain,
let love be brought to ignorance again.

The Wife And The Heart

The Wife: If he would only speak
and by invoking love
cause it to take the shape
that rocks the world once more;
if his too tranquil lips
could shed accomplishment
and shake the drowsy thing
out of its peaceful mist,
then, and by that sweet need,
would love exist.

The Heart: And if he spoke, what then?
Can you lay hands on words?
Can you be nursed and fed
and got with child by words?
His arm around your sleep
is truer than the drift
of what lacks blood and bone
and cannot stay, what clasps
the sky with sprays of fire
and, clasping, must expire.

The Wife: His arm is warm and strong,
a simple animal
that does not know its name
and has no name for death;
but words, expiring, fall
into the resonant mind
and give reality
a flower name that stands
four-seasoned, white and tall
and does not fall.

The Heart: And does not fall? Ah wife,
memory is false as spring
and tires of the same sun;

words, like the touch of flesh
going, leave you unstrung
with the old thirst again:
while sound returns to air
and matter blows apart,
I stay, your malady,
the sleepless heart.

In Memory Of Anton Webern,
Dead September 15, 1945

"On leaving the house of his son-in-law in Mittersill, near Salzburg, Anton Webern, 62-year-old Austrian composer of micromusically subtilized instrumental works, is accidentally killed by an American sentinel in consequence of his failure to obey a misinterpreted signal to stop."

Slonimsky, *Music since 1900*

Tinged leaves lie
on the Austrian earth, like scabs
closing wounds, and guns
are stacked with last summer's hay
in warm, dry places. Home
is again a room where a crackling fire
ripens late apples on the window sill
for a child's eventual pleasure:
so subtly does patience turn the years
and prove despair a changeling.
Women in shawls and men
with the simple minds of saints
stop at the wayside shrines
where Christ hangs dozenfold
from rusted nails, to gather
strength for the winter, as if
gathering armloads of fuel.
Yet he who coaxed
dissonant music out from behind those crude
crossings of common wood
is dead of the peace which made such intricate
    music
in his ears that night, is dead
of the deadly habit, is dead
of incomprehension, is dead.
May he rest easy in his fashion

of lightness, though the knuckle of our doubt
scrapes hard against his grave,
dredging his silence for the gold of purpose:
o there is hope that lambs of snow
will cover the wounded ground
with the simple charity
of whiteness one of these autumn nights,
muffling our mouths out of questions
after the sense of things.

In The Rag And
Bone Shop

Trade me, shopkeeper Yeats,
one filthy rag, one bone
that can make poetry
for all my jeweled bits.

It is not that I lack the nerve
for the long, close look
but substance, the hard grit
that bonds it tight with words.

Lately I have been plagued
by the covert phase of death,
the subtly hardening heart
and the slick eunuch face
turned bastions against love,
the shorn mind, pruned
of its adventurous branches,
clipped to a neat shape.

A rag to light a fire,
a bone to whistle on!
Proprietary, proud,
you flash your bones like feathers
and wave your sweat-soaked rags
come on, come on, come on
before my covetous eyes.

"The Expense Of Spirit In A Waste Of Shame"

Two-tone motels and unlit lovers' lanes,
the usual drinks, the stale, expected lines,
standard persuasions of the lips and hands,
the motions of delight, and all the time
the laughter of some demon in his ears.
Something is wrong: he blames the hour, the place,
forgetting he has been love's whipping boy
since rose-point fans were used as barricades,
before an age of women whose legs show
and who will answer simply yes or no.

To the lost dreamers, kissing in the woods
of their own legend, miracles are not new;
but he, bedroom agnostic, cannot see
with the clairvoyance of the faithful, who
blow on the spirit with the body's breath
and by that doubtless summoning of light
make good their heat. Shy of the test by fire,
he haunts the outskirts of the wilderness,
where charms, unblessed, are futile; in his brain
the tired demon sighs, *try try again.*

Come Hither

"The noise from the insects is so loud, that it may be heard even in a vessel anchored several hundred yards from shore; yet within the recesses of the forest a universal silence appears to reign."

Darwin, *The Voyage of the Beagle*

Color and sway and sound
are the lures of the barkers
that show us the way to the temple

lead us through flashy broods
of summer, through the rain,
through the steam that swaddles our thighs

past hotbeds of spotted tongues,
of green, beguiling fingers
and thin, shuddering throats

into the valley of dancers
changing to rivers to lovers
to mourners to clouds to grasses

and out again, deeper, deeper,
past the stump where the leopard screams
Beware of the shimmer of silence

to the burned-over hermitage
of a god whose broken eyes
harbor the golden bees

who smiles and smiles and smiles.

An Ancient Woman

I knew an ancient woman once
across a passage of despair
whose eyes were full of clouds, whose hair
was part and parcel of the dance

of light across the flesh of grass,
who said, "The other side of death
is easier on blood and breath
but o the wilderness you cross!"

Who said, "The passage of despair
lies between coveting and not,
between I shall and I forgot,
between the object and the air
that runs through bone-dry hands like sea.
Child, child, you need an angel there," said she.

DATE DUE